Stonybrook Junior High School

PICTURES BY BETTY FRASER

DODOS AND DINOSAURS

ISBN: 0 87191-038-1   Library of Congress Catalog Card Number: 73-104925

ARE EXTINCT

BY JULIAN MAY

CREATIVE EDUCATIONAL SOCIETY, INC.   MANKATO, MINNESOTA 56001

Once, on a faraway island in the Indian Ocean, there lived a strange bird. It could not fly because its wings were too small to lift its heavy body. The first men who saw it called the bird *dodo*, a word meaning "silly."

As years went by, the island settlers
brought dogs and pigs. These animals ate
the eggs and young of the dodos. The birds
began to disappear. Finally, only 200 years
after men had first seen the dodo, the last
of the birds died.

RESTORATION OF EXTINCT DODO

All that is left today is bones and the head and foot of a stuffed dodo. When all the animals of one kind disappear, that animal is said to be extinct. The dodo became extinct about the year 1681.

In the early days of America, great flocks of passenger pigeons filled the air. But then hunters killed many of them. And a great storm in 1881 destroyed millions of birds and eggs. The bird became extinct in 1914.

Another kind of pigeon, the rock dove, was brought to America from Europe. Once this bird lived among rocks. Today it nests on city buildings. This bird has not become extinct. There are more rock doves today than ever before.

HEATH HEN

Animals become extinct for many reasons. Some animals and birds that once lived in North America are extinct, or nearly so, because they could not live with man. Men hunted them; and men destroyed the places that were once the animals' homes.

CAROLINA PARAKEET

EASTERN BISON

GRAY SQUIRREL

OPOSSUM

Other animals were able to change their lives, or adapt, to man and his cities and farms. These animals, without any help from man, are more common than ever. Their adaptability has saved them.

COYOTE

	ONE-CELLED ANIMALS	SPONGES	JELLYFISH AND CORALS	MOLLUSKS
MODERN TIMES				
1 million years ago				
100 million years ago				
200 million years ago				
300 million years ago				
400 million years ago				
500 million years ago				
600-1,000 million years ago				

Man has caused some animals to become extinct. But man cannot be blamed for all extinct animals. Fossils, or traces in the rocks, show us that living things have been on earth for more than a billion years. And almost all of the creatures we know from fossils are extinct. Man did not cause this; he has only been on earth for about two million years. The real secret of extinction lies in the way that animals adapt.

JOINT-LEGGED ANIMALS	STARFISH	FISHES	AMPHIBIANS	REPTILES	BIRDS	MAMMALS	MAN	

TRILOBITES

Sometimes animals adapt by a change in body form. This doesn't happen because an animal "wants" to change. Rather, when animals reproduce, most of the young look and act like the parents. But there are often a few babies that are a bit different.

NAUTILOID

If the different body helps the animal to live
better, it will survive and have young of its
own. But if the different body is harmful,
the animal will not live. And more important,
it will produce no young like itself.

ANCIENT LUNGFISHES

A large group of animals, all of the same kind, is
called a population. A new population can grow from
one new animal. If the new animals have bodies that
are only a little better than the old kind, the new
population may grow slowly. Later, it may become extinct.

DINICHTHYS

But if the change helps the new population to take food from the old population, or to escape enemies better, then it will be the old group that becomes extinct. (A single animal is said to die. Only a whole population can become extinct.)

About 100 million years ago, most mammals had pouches to carry their young. Pouched animals were rather stupid, with small brains. Then more modern mammals appeared, without pouches and with larger brains. They took food and living space from the pouched mammals. This is called competing. In many parts of the world, pouched mammals became extinct.

EXTINCT OPOSSUM COMPETES WITH MORE MODERN MAMMAL FOR FOOD

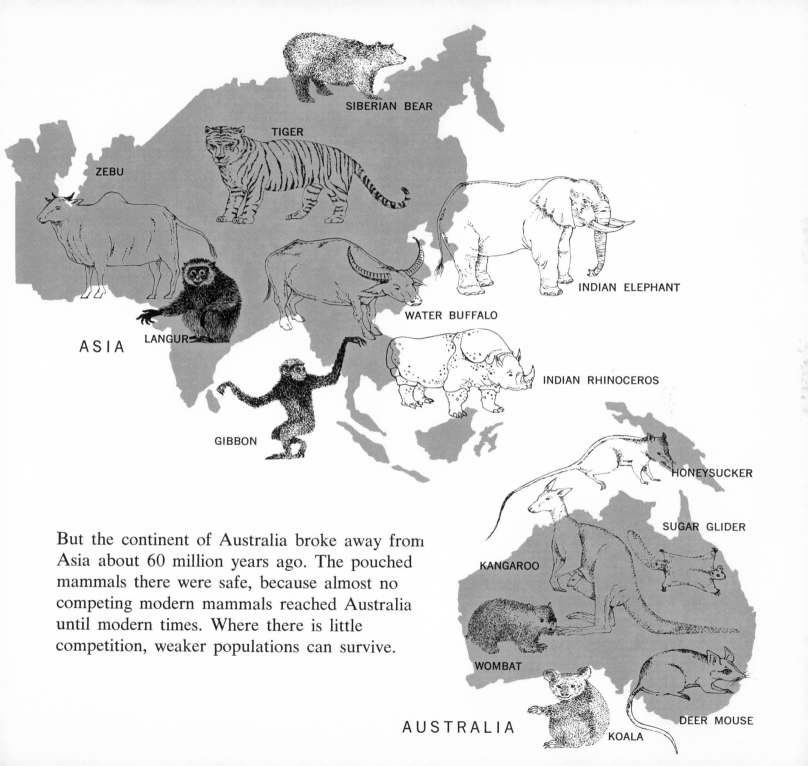

SIBERIAN BEAR

TIGER

ZEBU

INDIAN ELEPHANT

LANGUR

WATER BUFFALO

ASIA

INDIAN RHINOCEROS

GIBBON

HONEYSUCKER

SUGAR GLIDER

KANGAROO

But the continent of Australia broke away from Asia about 60 million years ago. The pouched mammals there were safe, because almost no competing modern mammals reached Australia until modern times. Where there is little competition, weaker populations can survive.

WOMBAT

DEER MOUSE

KOALA

AUSTRALIA

AMERICAN CHESTNUT

Extinction can happen because of disease.
Living things may adapt to the germs around
them. But if a disease is carried in from
far away, the living things may not be able
to adapt before becoming extinct. American
chestnut trees have nearly all died from
a disease that was brought from Asia.

Extinction can also happen when an animal's food supply disappears. The world's climate has changed many times. When it changes, some plants become extinct and so do the animals that feed on them. Hunting animals that feed on the plant-eaters must soon join the "parade of extinction."

Some extinctions are very puzzling. During
three times in the history of the world, there
have been rather sudden extinctions of many
animal populations. The first one we know about
happened about 230 million years ago.

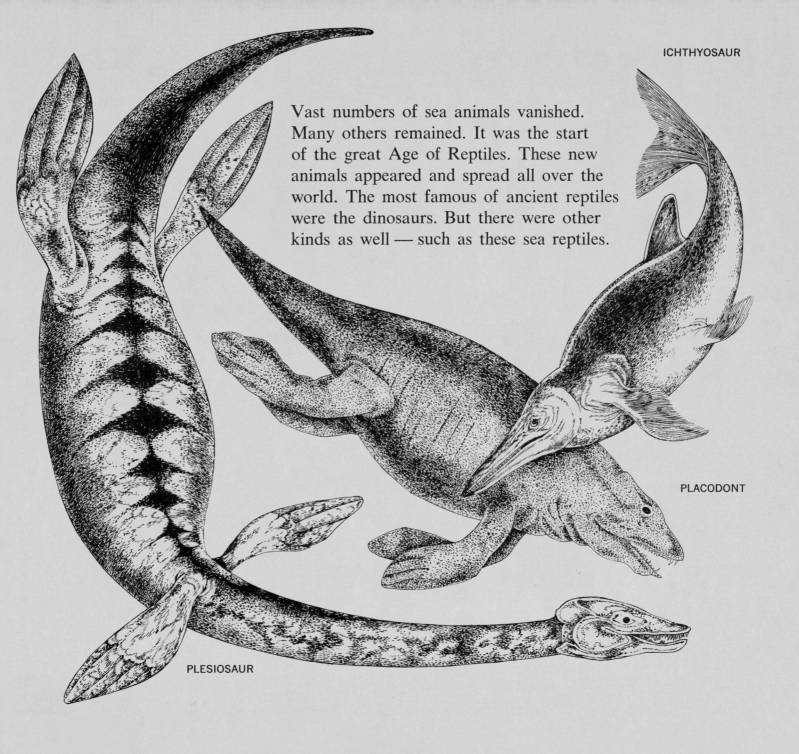

ICHTHYOSAUR

Vast numbers of sea animals vanished. Many others remained. It was the start of the great Age of Reptiles. These new animals appeared and spread all over the world. The most famous of ancient reptiles were the dinosaurs. But there were other kinds as well — such as these sea reptiles.

PLACODONT

PLESIOSAUR

DIPLODOCUS

COMPSOGNATHUS

Some reptiles were large and some small. There were gentle plant-eaters and fierce hunters. Populations evolved slowly, changing in body form. Many kinds slowly became extinct — for reasons you have already read about. But then a mysterious thing happened. About 60 million years ago there was a second "great dying" of many populations. It happened in a very short time, killing all the dinosaurs and many large reptiles of the sea and air. Smaller reptiles still lived, and so did birds, mammals, and other animals.

STEGOSAURUS

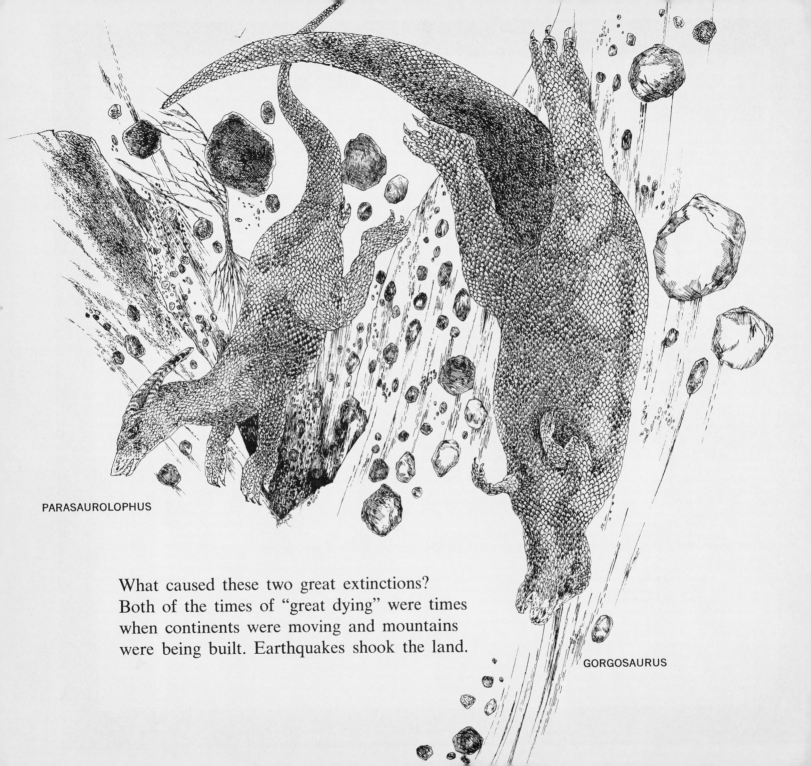

PARASAUROLOPHUS

GORGOSAURUS

What caused these two great extinctions?
Both of the times of "great dying" were times
when continents were moving and mountains
were being built. Earthquakes shook the land.

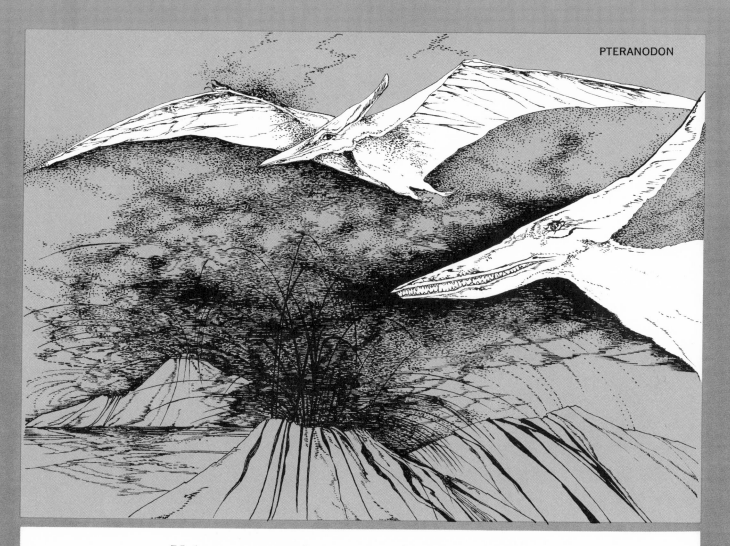

PTERANODON

Volcanoes poured gases into the air and chemicals
into the seas. Shallow seas became dry land.
The sun's light was dimmed by smoke and clouds.
There may have been great rainstorms.

ANATOSAURUS

Even small changes in the climate can bring
about the death of plants — both, in the sea
and on land. When certain plants became
extinct, the animals feeding on them had to
adapt to new food — or perish.

TYRANNOSAURUS   POUCHED RATS

Many large dinosaurs fed on swamp plants. They could not adapt to something else. When these dinosaurs became extinct, so did the giant meat-eaters that had hunted them. The hunters could not satisfy their hunger by catching small animals.

It was different for the smaller animals, such
as the mammals. They were more adaptable. Now
that the large reptiles were gone, the mammals
could survive better. There was more food.
There were fewer reptile enemies.

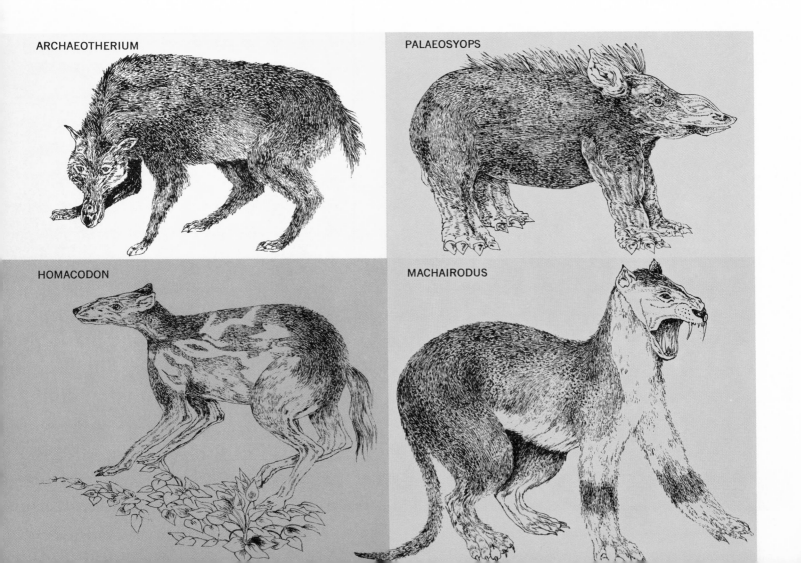

ARCHAEOTHERIUM

PALAEOSYOPS

HOMACODON

MACHAIRODUS

Much is still unknown about the first two times of "great dying." Why did the continents move and the mountains form? Some scientists think the sun might have caused it. Others think that the earth just changes as it grows older.

NOTHARCTUS   BRONTOTHERIUM   OROHIPPUS

There was a third, somewhat smaller, "great dying"
about 10,000 years ago. It took place toward the
end of the great Ice Age, when men still lived as
simple hunters and cave-dwellers.

In North America, more than 100 kinds of
giant mammals became extinct — mammoth,
mastodon, saber-tooth tiger, giant beaver,
giant wolf, and many others. Giant mammals
suddenly became extinct in other parts of
the world, too.

EUROPEAN CAVE BEAR

The end of the Ice Age was not a time of mountain-building. This could not have caused the extinctions. Disease might have killed some animal populations — but why did mostly large animals die?

The climate was changing 10,000 years ago. There were longer, colder winters but less rain and snow. Some scientists believe that this might have made it hard for larger mammals to care for their young.

WOOLLY RHINOCEROS

EXTINCT BISON

Others think that early man himself destroyed
the giant mammals. They could be killed by
chasing them over cliffs, or by setting huge
fires. This kind of hunting was very wasteful.

Many large animals of Africa did not disappear
in the third "great dying." Maybe the early
men in Africa were more skillful hunters, who
only took what they needed for food.

ELAND

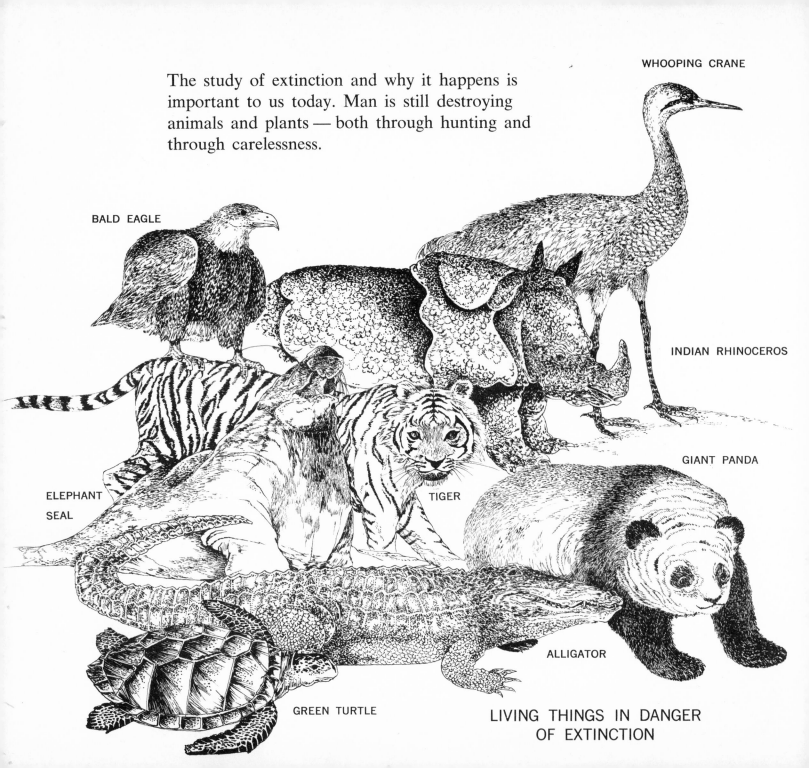

The study of extinction and why it happens is important to us today. Man is still destroying animals and plants — both through hunting and through carelessness.

WHOOPING CRANE

BALD EAGLE

INDIAN RHINOCEROS

GIANT PANDA

ELEPHANT SEAL

TIGER

ALLIGATOR

GREEN TURTLE

LIVING THINGS IN DANGER
OF EXTINCTION

Many beautiful and interesting birds, mammals, reptiles, and other living things will disappear forever unless man helps them to survive.

KOALA

ORANGUTAN

KUDU

TRUMPETER SWAN

THYLACINE

POLAR BEAR

SNOW LEOPARD

We must save the other living things of
Earth. We need them if we are to survive
ourselves. Without plants and animals,
mankind would become as extinct as the
dodos and dinosaurs.